BUG FACTS
A Young Explorer's Guide

Patricia Shapiro

Technical Editor: Daniel Summers

Illustrators: Jacquie Gallo, Jane Case, Jacqueline Forsyth

JANDERO MEDIA

BUG FACTS A Young Explorer's Guide

Second Printing

Copyright @ 2014 Jandero Media

All rights reserved. No part of this publication may be reproduced, photocopied, stored in an unauthorized retrieval system, or transmitted in any form or by any means – including but not limited to; electronic, photocopy, audio/video recording without the prior written permission of the copyright holder.

ISBN-13: 978-0615647272

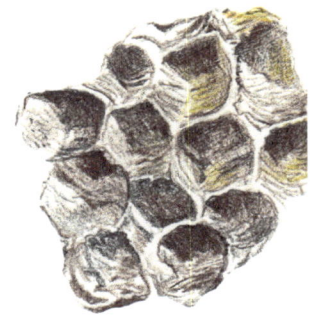

This book belongs to:

_____

ENTOMOLOGY: the study of insects.

Table of Contents

Insect Development 7
Insect Definition 8
Insects
    Boxelder (True Bug) 11
    Bumble Bee 12
    Cabbage Butterfly 13
    Cicada 14
    Click Beetle 15
    Common Black Ant 16
    Crane Fly 17
    Cricket 18
    Dragonfly 19
    Earwig 20
    Firefly (Lightning Bug) 21
    Flower Fly (Hover Fly) 22
    Giant Swallowtail Butterfly 23
    Grasshopper 24
    Harlequin Beetle 25
    Honey Bee 26
    Horse Fly 27
    House Fly 28
    Japanese Beetle 29
    June Bug 30
    Katydid 31

Ladybug	32
Luna Moth	33
Mayfly	34
Monarch Butterfly	35
Mosquito	36
Mud Dauber Wasp	37
Praying Mantis	38
Southern Fire Ant	39
Sphinx Moth	40
Stink Bug - Harlequin (True Bug)	41
Tiger Swallowtail Butterfly	42
Walking Stick	43
Water Backswimmer (True Bug)	44
Water Boatman (True Bug)	45
Water Strider (True Bug)	46
Yellow Jacket Wasp	47

Non-Insects

Centipede	51
Millipede	52
Pill Bug (Rolie Polie)	53

Checklist: What I have seen	55
Glossary	59
Reference	61

INSECT DEVELOPMENT

2 STAGE

Figure 1: The Pill Bug shown above is NOT an insect.

A two stage development cycle is called ametaboly. These insects look like small adults upon hatching. There are not many insects that go through a two-stage development cycle, though there are many other creatures in the animal kingdom that do.

3 STAGE

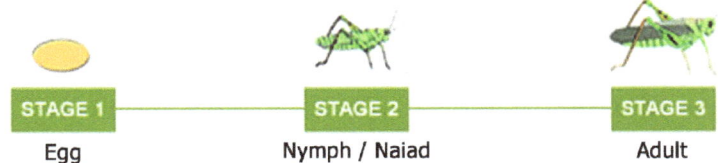

These three stage hatchlings look less like adults than their two-stage counterparts. This is called *Incomplete Metamorphosis*. On land, these young insects are called nymphs. If they live in the water they are called naiads. Molting (shedding of the skin) changes their appearance after the nymph/naiad stage. Young insects may have small wing buds, but they aren't noticeable until adulthood.

4 STAGE

Four-stage development involves a complete change in appearance between its larva stage and adulthood. This is called *Complete Metamorphosis*. During the pupa stage is when the insect's appearance changes the most.

INSECT DEFINITION

INSECT: small arthropods of the Insecta class that as an adult; have three pairs of legs and a body segmented into head, thorax, and abdomen. In their adult stage, these arthropods can also have up to two pairs of wings.

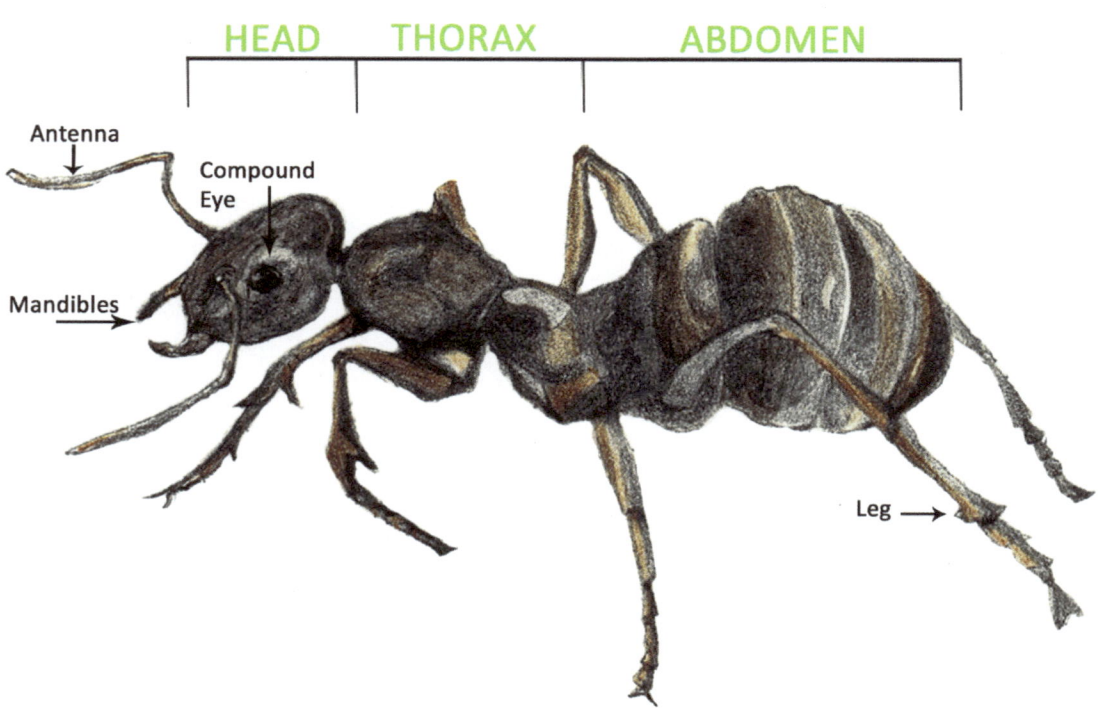

Insects

[What insect can be heard from a half mile away?]

Boxelder (True Bug)

MY HOME: On warm sunny days I like to warm myself in the sun, usually you will find me on the south and west sides of your house. I will only live in places that have a box elder or maple tree close by.

WHAT I EAT: I normally feed on the leaves and seedpods of the box elder tree or silver maple, but I cause little damage to the trees.

WHAT I LOOK LIKE: I am about ½ of an inch long, black body with three red lines just behind my head.

HOW I AM BORN: I go through three stages of development: egg, nymph and adult. My egg is laid on the leaves, branches, or trunk of the box elder tree. It takes only a few days for my egg to hatch and another 45 - 60 days to develop into an adult. I will hibernate during the winter and live about one year.

FUN FACTS: The boxelder lays its eggs almost exclusively on the female box elder tree, which produces the flowers and seeds during the spring. They are not harmful, just nuisance insects because they like to winter inside the warmth of a house. They can also be seen in the late summer under box elder trees by the thousands, getting prepared to hibernate.

Bumble Bee

MY HOME: I live in small nests and do not swarm. The queen will spend her entire life in the nest. The queen bumble bee will start building the nest when she is ready to lay eggs. She produces workers first to collect pollen.

WHAT I EAT: As an adult, I drink the nectar from flowers, or juices from fruit. I will only produce enough honey to feed the young bumblebees, which I store in honey pots.

WHAT I LOOK LIKE: I am ¾ of an inch in length, have four wings, a stinger at the end of my abdomen and am usually yellow and black in color. I appear to be 'furry' compared to other bees. I am bigger than a honey bee, but I am much less aggressive and usually will only attack if I feel my life is in danger.

HOW I AM BORN: Each spring the queen bee builds a nest out of wax. She deposits an egg in each cell and pollen for food, then seals up the cell. I hatch, go through larva and pupa stages, and develop into an adult worker bee, cutting my way out of the wax cell. This takes about 21 days.

FUN FACTS: If you find yourself in the presence of a bumble bee, just stand quietly. Once it realizes you're not a flower, it will move away. A bumble bee will not die if it uses its stinger.

CABBAGE BUTTERFLY

MY HOME: I am found in fields, gardens of North America, Africa, Asia, Australia and Europe.

WHAT I EAT: As a caterpillar, I will feed on cabbage, broccoli and other related crops, but if those are not available I will feed on native plants.

WHAT I LOOK LIKE: I am approximately two inches long and 1 ½ inches wide. I have a black body, white wings with black tips and black spots on my wings.

HOW I AM BORN: I will go through four stages of development: egg, caterpillar, chrysalis (cocoon), and adult (butterfly). My egg is laid on leaves or stems of plants. Once I hatch from the egg, I become a caterpillar. I will remain a caterpillar for a few weeks, eating most of the time to grow bigger and stronger. When it is time, I make myself a chrysalis (cocoon). I will emerge from that in a few weeks as a butterfly!

FUN FACTS: The cabbage butterfly originated in Europe and was introduced to North America in the mid-1800s.

Cicada

MY HOME: I am found in North America and throughout other parts of the world. I spend most of my life underground as a nymph. For the month I am an adult, I can be found on trees, plants, fences, houses and almost anywhere.

WHAT I EAT: As a nymph, I suck the sap from the roots of trees. As an adult, I have piercing sucking mouthparts and drink the juices from plant stems.

WHAT I LOOK LIKE: I have transparent wings that can have many patterns or colors, red eyes with a black body and will grow up to be about 3 inches long.

HOW I AM BORN: I go through three stages of development: egg, nymph and adult. My egg is laid in tree branches and when I hatch I fall to the ground. In my larval stage I am called a nymph and I can live in the ground for many years. Some periodic broods or nests of cicada larvae live in the ground for 17 years! I emerge from the ground and attach myself to trees, plants, or structures until I pop out of my skin and become an adult. As an adult, I only live from 2 weeks to 40 days.

FUN FACTS: You can hear the cicada's song for up to ½ mile away and they only sing during the daytime. The cicada makes the loudest sound of any insect. There are approximately 2,500 cicada species in the world.

Click Beetle

My home: I am found all over the world in warm climates and in areas of high vegetation. I am nocturnal and am attracted to lights.

What I eat: As a larva, I will eat the roots of plants. As an adult, I drink the nectar from flowers.

What I look like: I am brown in color and from ¼ to ¾ of an inch in length. I have a hinge across my body that allows me to flex. If I fall on my back I will flex, which makes me fly up in the air and produces the clicking sound. I will also 'click' to scare off predators.

How I am born: I go through four stages of development: egg, larva, pupa and adult. The female lays her eggs at the base of plants. Once my egg hatches into larva, I will live up to four years in this stage before I turn into an adult. Both adults and larvae will hibernate in the ground during the winter.

Fun Facts: Click beetles are very good at 'playing dead' to be less interesting to a bird or other predator, and will pretend they are dead for hours at a time.

Common Black Ant

MY HOME: I live in a colony, which can be in an anthill in the ground, a rotted log, an infested structure such as the foundation of a home or tree.

WHAT I EAT: My jaws open sideways like scissors. I cannot eat 'whole' food, but instead use my jaws to squeeze out the juice and throw away the hull. I eat almost anything, from other insects to vegetation.

WHAT I LOOK LIKE: I have six legs and two eyes: which are made up of many smaller eyes (or lenses). I have two stomachs: the first for my food, the second I use to feed other ants. I have two antennae that I use for smell and touch. The queen ant has wings and so do the male ants, both for a short time.

HOW I AM BORN: I have four stages of development: egg, larva, pupa and adult. The queen in my ant colony lays thousands of eggs. Worker ants take care of my egg until it hatches. I will live 45 to 60 days.

FUN FACTS: An ant can lift 10 to 20 times its own body weight. If a man weighed 180 pounds, he would have to lift 1,800 to 3,600 pounds to be as strong as an ant. Ants have the largest brain of any insect. The combined brain cells of a colony of ants have about the same number of brain cells as a human.

Crane Fly

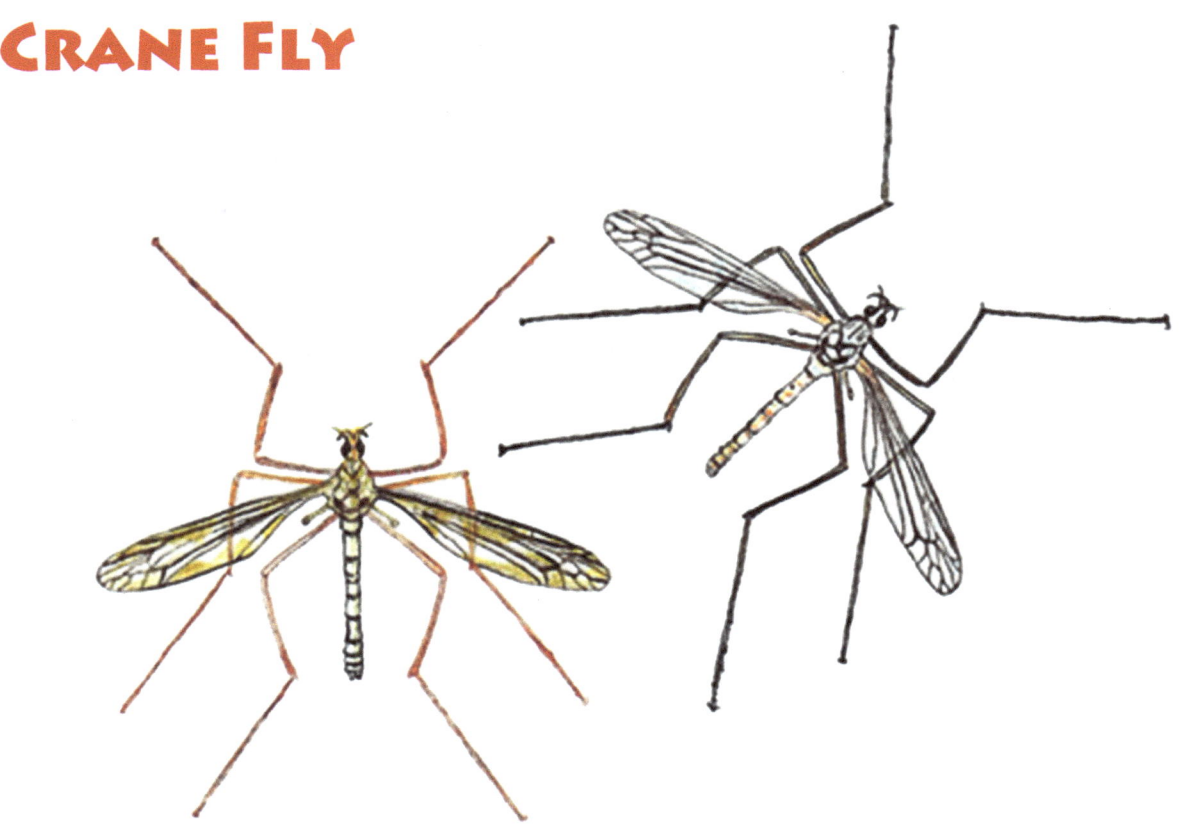

MY HOME: I am generally found around damp places and am attracted to light. As a larva, I usually live in damp habitats and sometimes I live in water.

WHAT I EAT: As a larva, I eat roots and other organic matter. I don't eat as an adult.

WHAT I LOOK LIKE: I am about 1 inch long, have six long spindly legs, a long thin body and am sometimes mistaken for a large mosquito.

HOW I AM BORN: I go through four stages of development: egg, larva, pupa and adult. My egg is laid in water, on water plants, moist soil or sometimes in rotted roofs. It takes 72 hours for my egg to hatch and about a month for me to become an adult. As an adult, I will only live for a few days, long enough to mate and lay new eggs.

FUN FACTS: In Europe I am called 'Daddy Long Legs'. I am commonly mistaken for a large mosquito.

CRICKET

MY HOME: I am found in North America and throughout other parts of the world. During the warm summer months I am found in fields, beneath rocks, or under some other yard debris.

WHAT I EAT: I feed on plants and sometimes other insects.

WHAT I LOOK LIKE: I am related to the grasshopper and the katydid. I am approximately one inch in length, have great vision and with my compound eyes can see in many different directions at once. My wings are usually too small to allow me to fly. If I am a male cricket, I can use my wings to make a chirping song instead.

HOW I AM BORN: I go through three stages of development: egg, nymph and adult. My egg is laid in the soil during the fall. When spring arrives my egg hatches. As a new cricket I look like a small adult. I grow each time I shed my skin (molt). I will live for about one year.

FUN FACTS: In many parts of the world, crickets are thought to bring good luck. It is rumored that crickets can tell the outside temperature: Count the number of chirps they make in one minute, divide by 4 and then add the number 40 to reach the outside temperature. There are about 900 species of crickets worldwide.

DRAGONFLY

MY HOME: I am most often found near water and usually remain within a few miles of the place where my egg was hatched.

WHAT I EAT: As a larva, I eat tadpoles or small fish. As an adult I will eat other small insects, primarily mosquitoes, and I am considered useful for controlling the mosquito population. Dragonflies are carnivorous in both larval and adult stages.

WHAT I LOOK LIKE: I can be any color and range in size by species from one to five inches. My antennae are very short.

HOW I AM BORN: I go through three stages of development: egg, naiad (larval) and adult. My egg is laid in water and I typically hatch in two to three weeks. In my larval stage I am called a naiad. I live in the water and use internal gills to breathe. I can live in the water as a naiad for two to three years. When I am ready to become an adult I crawl out of the water and shed my skin. As an adult, I can live for over a year if I migrate away from the cold.

FUN FACTS: The largest living dragonfly lived over 250 million years ago (before the dinosaurs) and had a wingspan of over three feet! A dragonfly needs warmth to fly and you will notice they will often land when the sun goes behind a cloud. There are 3,600 species of dragonfly in the world.

EARWIG

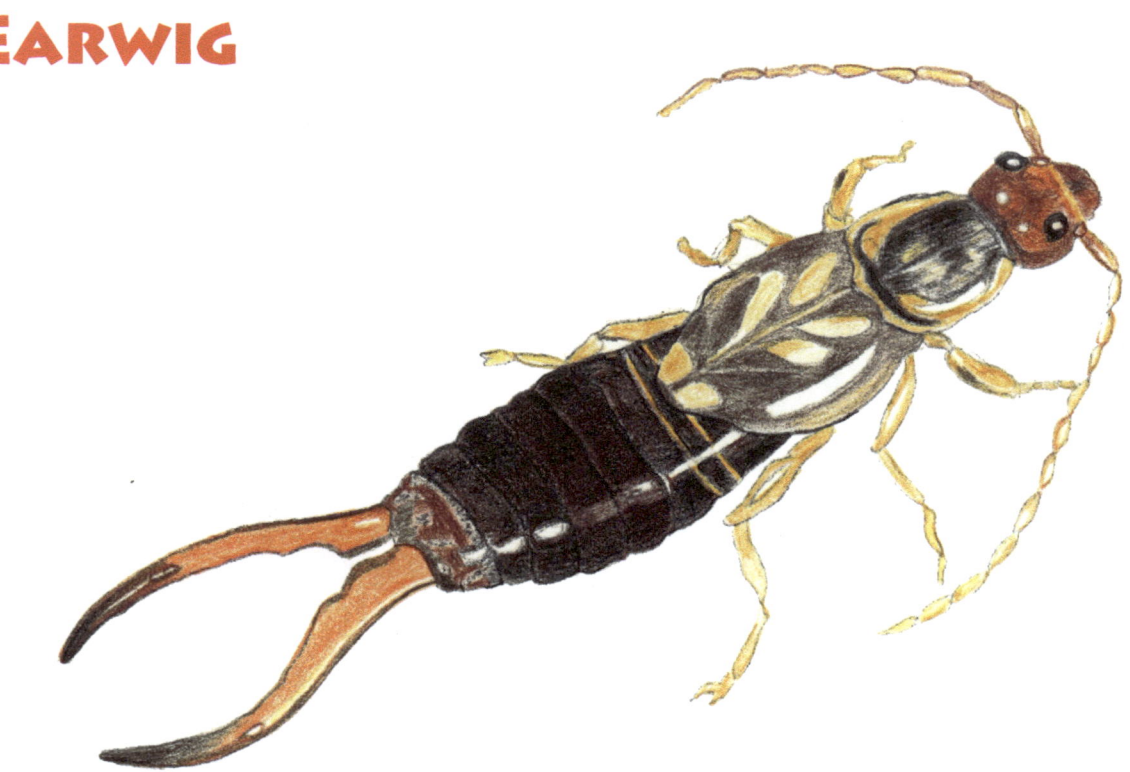

MY HOME: I prefer dark, moist environments and you can find me under logs, bark, leaves or hibernating during the winter in your home. I am usually only active at night unless disturbed.

WHAT I EAT: I eat both live and decaying plant material as well as live and dead insects.

WHAT I LOOK LIKE: I am dark brown, ½ to 3 inches long and have a set of pinchers located at the end of my body. The pinchers are used as a weapon and I may try to pinch if picked up.

HOW I AM BORN: I go through three stages of development: egg, nymph and adult. I lay from 30 to 50 eggs in a batch. It takes up to three months from the time the eggs are laid until I become an adult earwig.

FUN FACTS: Earwig received its name due to the myth the earwig would crawl into your ear if you slept on the ground. There are over 1,700 species of Earwigs in the world.

Firefly (Lightning Bug)

My home: I am found in humid, warm areas of the world, most often in rotting wood, by the edges of stream, ponds, drainage ditches or in some other moist area. The greatest numbers of fireflies are found in Asia and South America.

What I eat: As a larva, I eat earthworms, snails and slugs. As an adult, I eat pollen or other insects.

What I look like: I am approximately ¾ of an inch long, and I usually am black with two red spots on my head, with my outer casing outlined in yellow.

How I am born: I go through four stages of development: egg, larva, pupa and adult. The eggs are deposited in the ground and hatch in about a month. As a larva, I feed all summer long and hibernate during the winter. The next summer, I emerge and in about six weeks become an adult. Some species can live for several years by hibernating as larva during the winter.

Fun Facts: In the late evening the firefly will 'flash' a yellowish light to communicate with other fireflies. The males will flash approximately every five seconds and the females will flash approximately every two seconds. Many fireflies do not produce light.

Flower Fly (Hover Fly)

My Home: I am most commonly found in fields, crops, gardens and weedy areas. I am found on almost all of North America and throughout the world.

What I Eat: As a larva, I will eat aphids or other insect pests and also some plants. As an adult, I drink the nectar of flowers or fruit.

What I Look Like: Most people think that I am a bee, but I am indeed part of the fly family. My appearance is a natural defense so birds and other predators will not eat me. Usually I am bright yellow and black striped. I am also called a Hover Fly.

How I am Born: I go through four stages of development: egg, larva, pupa and adult. My egg is laid on a leaf that contains aphids and I hatch in two to three days. It takes about 25 to 30 days from egg to adulthood. I will live for only a few weeks once I am an adult.

Fun Facts: You can distinguish a flower fly from a bee by the number of wings; a fly has two wings, while bees have four.

Giant Swallowtail Butterfly

My Home: I am found throughout North America, and as far south as South America. In the southern states, I am seen most often around the citrus trees.

What I Eat: As a caterpillar, I will only eat leaves from citrus trees and prefer the new growth leaves. As an adult I drink the nectar from flowers.

What I Look Like: My wings are 4 to 7 inches in width from the top tips of my wings, and the females are larger than the males. I have black wings with yellow horizontal stripes. I have a long thin black body with two antennae.

How I Am Born: I will go through four stages of development: egg, larva (caterpillar), pupa (chrysalis), and adult (butterfly). After eating most of the time and getting bigger, I form a chrysalis that is attached to the citrus branch with small strong silken threads. I will emerge as a butterfly and can produce two to three generations a year.

Fun Facts: When Swallowtail caterpillars feel threatened, they have an orange gland that they stick out, exuding a *terrible* smell!

GRASSHOPPER

MY HOME: I am found in gardens, fields, on crops and forests in almost all climates worldwide.

WHAT I EAT: I am an herbivore, which means I eat only plants.

WHAT I LOOK LIKE: I come in many sizes and up to 5 inches in length. I can walk, hop great distances and even fly. I have five eyes and no ears, but can still hear with a special organ on my abdomen called a tympanal organ. My large back legs are used for hopping and making music. My smaller front legs are used for eating and walking.

HOW I AM BORN: I go through three stages of development: egg, nymph and adult. My egg is laid in the fall and will hatch during the spring. I hatch into a nymph, which looks like an adult grasshopper, but without wings. I shed my skin many times to grow. When I become an adult I have developed wings. I will live about one year.

FUN FACTS: They make their sound (music) by rubbing their wings or legs together. They can jump 20 times the length of their body. That would be like a 6' man jumping 120 feet. There are over 18,000 different species worldwide.

Harlequin Beetle

My home: I am native to the Americas and found in warm climates, primarily Central and South America. I am a type of long-horned beetle, active during the day, but can be found around lights at night.

What I eat: I feed on the sap from trees.

What I look like: I have black, yellow and red markings. I can grow up to 3 inches in length. If I am a male Harlequin Beetle, my forelegs can be longer than my entire body. Even with these long forelegs, I can crawl as well as fly.

How I am born: I go through four stages of development (complete metamorphosis): egg, larva, pupa and adult. If I am a female beetle, I will lay my eggs in the bark of a tree and can lay up to 20 eggs at a time. Once my egg hatch into larva, they will bury into the wood where they will remain for up to 8 months. They will pupate in the wood and emerge after another 4 months. It will take almost a year to become an adult beetle.

Fun Facts: Harlequin beetles often have tiny arachnids, known as pseudo scorpions, living under their wing covers. These pseudo scorpions use the beetles as a mode of transportation much like people use a bus.

Honey Bee

MY HOME: I am a social insect and live in large colonies, usually in hives and with up to 80,000 individuals. I do not hibernate during the winter, but group together and use community warmth to stay alive. I am found worldwide.

WHAT I EAT: I drink nectar from flowers or juices from fruit. An average hive yields 50 pounds of honey, which is my food during the winter. To make one pound of honey requires the nectar from millions of flowers.

WHAT I LOOK LIKE: Usually less than ¾ of an inch in length and have four wings. I am usually golden brown in color with black stripes on my abdomen. I have a stinger at the end of my abdomen.

HOW I AM BORN: I go through four stages of development: egg, larva, pupa and adult. The queen bee lays eggs and the worker bees will take care of my egg until I hatch. I will stay with the hive usually for the rest of my life.

FUN FACTS: Honeybees are the only insects that produce a food that is consumed by humans. They provide people with honey, bee's wax and pollinate crops. They communicate with each other using a 'dance' language. A honeybee will die if it uses its stinger.

Horse Fly

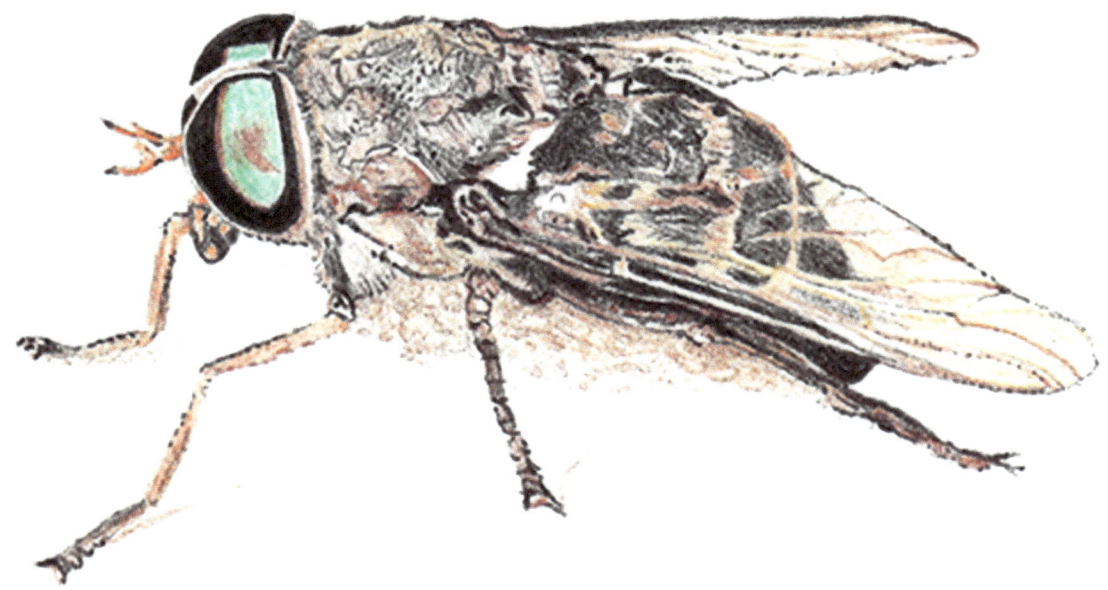

MY HOME: I am generally found near areas that contain water and also close to livestock areas, which is a food source.

WHAT I EAT: As a larva, I eat other insects, worms, snails and occasionally a small fish. If I am an adult female, I will drink the blood of large animals and humans. If I am a male adult, I will only drink nectar from flowers or juices from fruit.

WHAT I LOOK LIKE: I am up to 1 ¼ inches in length. I can have grey, black, or a brown body and my two wings are generally dark colored. I resemble a housefly, but am larger and have short horn shaped antennae.

HOW I AM BORN: I go through four stages of development: egg, larva, pupa and adult. My egg is laid on plants in or near water. Once I hatch, as a larva I will spend one to two years growing in moist soil or water. As an adult, I only live for a few days.

FUN FACTS: If a horse or deer fly lands on you and bites, it is a female fly. There are approximately 3,000 species of horse flies world-wide; 350 in North America alone!

House Fly

MY HOME: I am the most common of all flies and always found in the company of humans, human activities or homes. I am inactive at night.

WHAT I EAT: As a larva, I eat organic material like plants, food or juices in trash cans. As an adult, I can only drink liquids, usually the juices of decaying or sweet substances.

WHAT I LOOK LIKE: I have two eyes, but there are over 4,000 smaller 'eyes' in each main eye. I am usually black with transparent wings and up to ¼ inch long.

HOW I AM BORN: I go through four stages of development: egg, larva, pupa and adult. I fully develop in only about 10 days. Females can lay 2,500 eggs in just a month. As an adult fly, I live from around 30 to 60 days.

FUN FACTS: Flies use their antennae to smell. A fly can go 45 mph and beat its wings up to 200 times per second. Houseflies existed 65 million years ago!

Japanese Beetle

MY HOME: I am found in almost all parts of the United States, Asia, Europe and Canada and live in fields, crops, and in backyards.

WHAT I EAT: I eat around 300 species of plants, even poison ivy. I usually will feed with a group of other beetles. We start at the top of a plant and work our way down. We can be very destructive to crops when large groups of us are hungry. I eat the soft tissue out between the veins of the leaves and cause the leaf to look skeletonized.

WHAT I LOOK LIKE: As an adult I am ½ to ¾ of an inch in length. I have hard metallic green shells with copper colored wing casings.

HOW I AM BORN: I go through four stages of development: egg, larva, pupa and adult. My egg is laid in the ground in the fall and I emerge in spring, usually late May. I will live for 30 - 45 days as an adult.

FUN FACTS: Japanese beetles can fly as far as five miles, but are poor fliers and can be caught easily. When approached, they lift their spiny hind legs up in the air to scare off the intruder.

JUNE BUG

MY HOME: Found all over North America, I hide in trees during the day. As adult beetles, we swarm in great numbers in early summer, usually at dark and are strongly attracted to lights.

WHAT I EAT: As a larva, I live underground and eat the roots of grasses and other plants. As an adult, I feed at night and eat vegetation, usually the leaves from trees and bushes.

WHAT I LOOK LIKE: I am less than one inch in length, am dark brown to blackish in color, have a hard casing and have wings.

HOW I AM BORN: I go through four stages of development: egg, larva, pupa and adult. My egg is laid in the ground, and I can live for two to three years in the ground as a larva before surfacing to become an adult. My total lifespan is up to four years.

FUN FACTS: June bugs get their name from emerging in great quantities in June. These beetles make a tasty food for your pet toads and lizards.

KATYDID

MY HOME: I can be found on branches of trees or bushes in North America and other parts of the world. I am most active at night and sing in the evening. There are many species of katydids, commonly found throughout the southern part of the United States.

WHAT I EAT: I eat leaves, flowers, the stems, and fruits of many plants and a few species of katydids are predators and will eat other insects.

WHAT I LOOK LIKE: I am usually green and range in size by species from 1 to 5 inches. My antennae are two or three times the length of my body.

HOW I AM BORN: I go through three stages of development: egg, nymph and adult. My egg is laid in the fall on plants or in the soil and I hatch in the spring. Once I hatch as a nymph, I look like adults except without wings. I shed my skin (molt) to grow. As an adult I will have developed my wings. My lifespan is about one year from egg to the end of adulthood.

FUN FACTS: Katydids get their name from how their song sounds: "Katy did, Katy didn't." They rub their wings together to produce their song sound, which serves as part of their courtship. Their ears tympana (hearing organs) are on their front legs.

LADYBUG

MY HOME: I am found all over the world and live in a variety of places including gardens, forests, fields and grasslands.

WHAT I EAT: As a larva, I can eat over 25 aphids a day. Once I am grown to an adult, I can eat over 50 aphids a day.

WHAT I LOOK LIKE: I am around ¼ of an inch long and am usually yellow, orange or red with black spots on my wing covers. I also have black legs, head and antennae. The number of black spots I might have will vary by individual ladybug. My black spots will fade as I get older.

HOW I AM BORN: I go through four stages of development: egg, larva, pupa and adult. My tiny yellow egg is laid on a leaf and will hatch in about a week. When I hatch, I am in a worm like larva stage for almost a month. I finally get strong enough to pupate and become an adult. I can hibernate during the winter and live around one year.

FUN FACTS: A ladybug's wings beat over 80 times a second in flight. Ladybugs will play dead when threatened. In 1999, four ladybugs were sent into space on NASA's Columbia space shuttle.

Luna Moth

My Home: I am found in trees of the eastern part of the United States and into Canada. I only fly at night and that is how I got my name, the word "luna" means moon.

What I Eat: As a caterpillar, I will eat hickory, sycamore and walnut leaves. I do not have a mouth and do not eat as an adult.

What I Look Like: My wings are light green with yellow stripes that have a long wing tail. My wingspan is approximately five inches long and four inches wide. I am one of the largest moths in North America.

How I Am Born: I will go through four stages of development: egg, caterpillar, pupa (cocoon), and adult. The female can lay 400 to 600 eggs, four to six eggs at a time on the underside of leaves. It can take up to two weeks for my egg to hatch into a lime green caterpillar with small orange spots along the sides. It takes about six weeks from the time my egg is laid to turn into an adult.

Fun Facts: The adult Luna Moth does not have a mouth, which is why they only live about a week. Luna Moths are members of the giant silkworm family.

MAYFLY

MY HOME: I will spend most of my life as a larva in the water. I am found throughout North America and in most parts of the world.

WHAT I EAT: As a larva, I eat algae. As an adult, I cannot eat because I do not have a functional mouth.

WHAT I LOOK LIKE: I am usually green, ½ to 1 inch in length and have two or three long tails that extend from the end of my body. I have two sets of wings that are held up over my body when I am not flying.

HOW I AM BORN: I go through three stages of development: egg, naiad and adult. My egg is laid in the water. I will hatch into a naiad and spend up to three years living in the water. As an adult, I will only live from two minutes to two days, only long enough to reproduce.

FUN FACTS: Mayflies have been around since before dinosaurs even existed; over 350 million years. Mayflies need clean water to live in and scientists look for their larva in water to see if the water is polluted.

Monarch Butterfly

MY HOME: I am found on all continents except the polar region. I migrate great distances in the winter, from Canada all the way to Mexico.

WHAT I EAT: As a caterpillar, I will only eat the leaves and stems of the milkweed plant. As an adult, I drink the nectar from flowers or the juices from fruit.

WHAT I LOOK LIKE: My wings are approximately three inches from tip to tip and my body is about one inch long. I have a black body and my wings are orange, yellow with black lines running thru them. The edges of my wings have a black border with white spots.

HOW I AM BORN: I will go through four stages of development: egg, caterpillar, chrysalis (cocoon), and adult (butterfly). The female Monarch can lay up to 400 eggs on the leaves or stems of the milkweed plant. I am hatched from an egg and become a caterpillar. After a few weeks of eating and getting bigger, I make my chrysalis). It takes me a few more weeks before I emerge as a butterfly.

FUN FACTS: Each year monarch butterflies fly up to 2,000 miles from northeastern North America to Mexico. Recent tests show that Monarchs navigate using the earth's magnetic field.

Mosquito

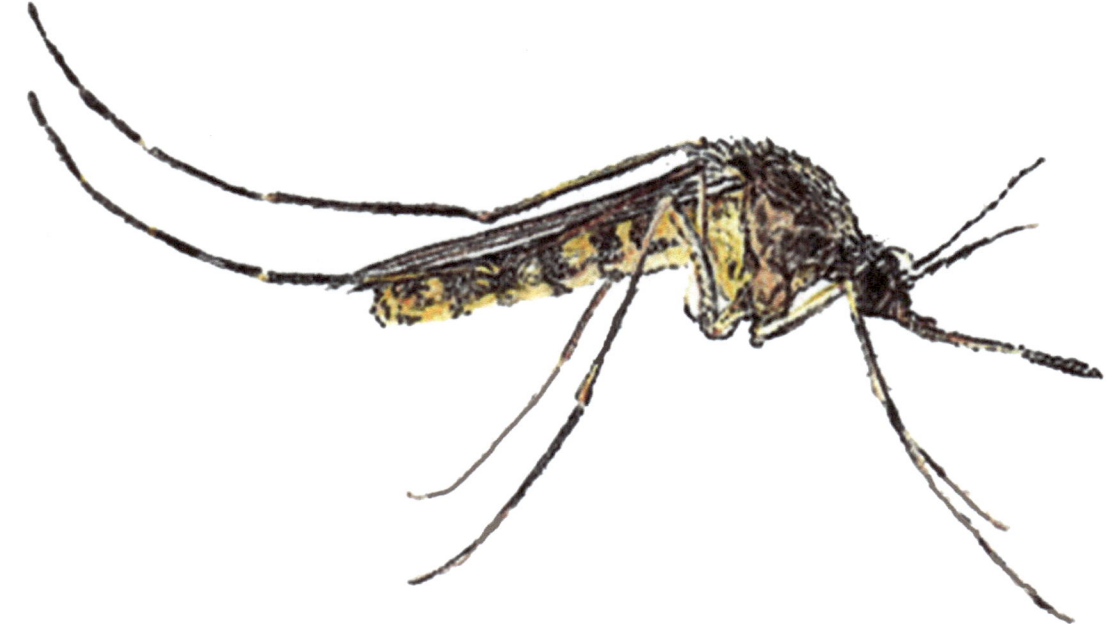

MY HOME: I will usually remain within one mile of the place where my egg hatched. I am found most often near a water source; rivers, ponds, lakes, streams or pools of standing water.

WHAT I EAT: As a larva, I eat the organic material in the water. As an adult male mosquito, I will drink the nectar or juices from decaying materials. As an adult female mosquito, I will need to drink blood because I require a blood meal to develop my eggs.

WHAT I LOOK LIKE: I am ½ to ¾ of an inch in length, gray in color with a long needle like mouth part that is used to drink my food.

HOW I AM BORN: I go through four stages of development: egg, larva, pupa and adult. A female will lay her eggs in water, 100 to 300 at a time. As a larva in the water, I breathe by using a tube I stick up above the surface like a snorkel. My life cycle from egg to adult is about a month. Female mosquitoes live up to 100 days. The males only live approximately 20 days.

FUN FACTS: Mosquitoes existed about 170 million years ago, during the time of the dinosaurs. There are about 3,500 mosquito species worldwide.

Mud Dauber Wasp

My home: I am a solitary wasp; I do not fly in a swarm of wasps or live in large colonies. During the summer months you can usually find me collecting mud for my nests.

What I eat: I eat other insects.

What I look like: I am long and thin with a thread like waist, around ½ to 1 inch in length. I can be black and yellow striped or blackish blue in color and have a stinger located at the end of my abdomen.

How I am born: I go through four stages of development: egg, larva, pupa and adult. My nest is built out of mud, which can contain up to 25 eggs. Each cell of the mud nest contains an insect (usually spiders) plus one egg, and is sealed up with mud. After only a few days, my egg hatches. As a larva, I will eat the insect put in the mud cell with me for food. I remain a larva for about three weeks, and spin a cocoon in the cell. I usually remain in the cocoon over the winter and emerge in the spring from the cell as an adult wasp. My life span is about one year.

Fun Facts: If you see a large quantity of mud dauber nests close together, that usually is just the work of one female. Mud daubers are not as aggressive as yellow jackets, and they can sting repeatedly without dying.

Praying Mantis

My home: I am found in warm climates on bushes, trees, houses or any structure where I can find another insect for a meal.

What I eat: I eat other insects.

What I look like: I can be green or brown, and range 2 to 3 inches in length. I have a triangular shaped head with a long torso and grasshopper type back legs. My front legs have spines and are held upright when I am still, which makes it look like I am praying.

How I am born: I go through three stages of development: egg, nymph and adult. The female lays an egg case in the fall that contains up to 300 eggs. I hatch in the spring and emerge as a nymph, resembling a miniature adult, except without wings. I will develop into an adult by molting, shedding my skin. As an adult, my lifespan is less than a year.

Fun Facts: They are the only insects that can turn their head side-to-side 180 degrees. Their eyes can see movement up to 60 feet away. The praying mantis bites the back of the neck of its victim to paralyze it before eating it. There are over 1,500 species of the praying mantis worldwide.

Southern Fire Ant

My Home: I am found burrowing in the ground, under structures, around fireplaces and in the foundations of homes. There are many species of fire ants, commonly found throughout the southern part of the United States.

What I Eat: My menu includes; plants, nectar, seeds, other insects and meat from dead animals.

What I Look Like: I can come in several sizes. Worker ants can be 1/16 to 1/3 of an inch in size. Winged and queen ants are slightly larger. My body is reddish brown and my abdomen is black.

How I Am Born: I have four stages of development: egg, larva, pupa and adult. The queen lays her eggs in the nest and the worker ants care for them. The queen can lay up to 800 eggs a day. It takes 30 to 35 days for my egg to develop into an adult. The queen ant can live for up to seven years. A worker ant lives an average of five weeks.

Fun Facts: They usually swarm in late spring or early summer. The population of one ant colony averages 100,000 to 500,000 ants. They will sting and bite an intruder and should not be touched. There are over 250 species of fire ants worldwide.

Sphinx Moth

MY HOME: I am found throughout the world. I primarily hide during the day and emerge at dusk or during the early morning hours.

WHAT I EAT: As a caterpillar, I eat the leaves and stems of plants. As an adult moth, I am a nectarivore and feed on the nectar from flowers. I will go from flower to flower hovering over them and I am often confused with the hummingbird.

WHAT I LOOK LIKE: As a caterpillar, I am green and have a pointed 'horn' on my rear end. As an adult moth, I have a long narrow set of front wings and a shorter set of back wings. My wingspan can be 2 to 8 inches from tip to tip.

HOW I AM BORN: I will go through four stages of development: egg, caterpillar, pupa (cocoon), and adult. Females lay as many as 1,000 eggs on leaves. My egg will hatch in two to three days as a caterpillar. It takes me about eight weeks to go from egg to full grown caterpillar. Then I burrow into the ground to pupate. The common sphinx will over winter underground as a pupa and hatch out in the early summer. In tropical or warmer regions, it can take only two to three weeks to hatch out of the ground and broods are produced all year long.

FUN FACTS: All sphinx moths have the ability to hover due to their size and rapid wing beats. People often mistake the protrusion on the back of the sphinx caterpillar for a stinger.

Stink Bug - Harlequin (True Bug)

My Home: I am commonly found on crop plants such as; turnips, cauliflower, cabbage and also fruit trees.

What I Eat: I drink the juices from fruits and plants with my piercing mouth parts.

What I Look Like: My outside is a hard case, greenish and flattened with a shield shape that is about ¼ to ½ of an inch long. I emit an unpleasant (stinky) smell as a method of defense.

How I am Born: I am a type of 'True Bug' and go through three stages of development: egg, young adult and adult. The female lays a double row of eggs on stems or leaves in the fall and I hatch in the spring. It takes me about 35 days to become an adult after my egg is laid.

Fun Facts: Certain types of stink bugs are used as food by humans in parts of Africa, Mexico and India. There are over 5,000 species of stink bugs worldwide.

Tiger Swallowtail Butterfly

My Home: I am found throughout North America, from Canada all the way to Mexico.

What I Eat: As a caterpillar, I am a very picky eater and usually will only eat leaves from the wild cherry or tulip trees. As an adult I will drink the nectar from flowers.

What I Look Like: My wings are four to five inches in width, four inches in height and are usually yellow and black striped. I have a long thin black body with two antennae.

How I Am Born: I will go through four stages of development: egg, caterpillar, chrysalis (cocoon), and adult (butterfly). My egg is laid on or close to a cherry or tulip tree. I hatch from the egg and become a caterpillar for a few weeks. After eating most of the time and getting bigger, I form a chrysalis (cocoon). I will emerge as a butterfly in a few weeks.

Fun Facts: Swallowtails have two wing tails that hang down at the bottom of their wings. Often, they will lose one of their wing 'tails' to a predatory bird, but they can still fly.

Walking Stick

My Home: I am usually found on bushes or in small trees. I look like a twig and part of the plant I am on so I can hide from birds and other predators. My specialty is camouflage.

What I Eat: I only eat leaves and stems of plants and usually only eat at night.

What I Look Like: My size ranges from less than 1 inch to over 1 foot in length, depending on my species. I have a built in camouflage and appear to look like part of the plant.

How I am Born: I go through three stages of development: egg, nymph and adult. The female can lay up to 150 eggs, dropping them one by one to the ground. My egg is also camouflaged and resembles a brown seed. I hatch in the spring as a nymph and resemble a tiny adult. My lifespan is one season.

Fun Facts: The walking stick has the ability to regenerate lost limbs. A female can reproduce by herself, but will only produce other females. Some species of walking sticks can squirt a fluid that will make their potential predators temporarily blind.

Water Backswimmer (True Bug)

MY HOME: I am often confused with the Water Boatman insect; but unlike the boatman insect, I can give a stinging painful bite. The easiest way to tell us apart is I swim on my back (upside down). I am found in freshwater ponds, slow moving streams and lakes.

WHAT I EAT: I eat other insects, small fish and even tadpoles. I have tube shaped piercing mouth parts. I use my short front legs to grab and attack my prey with a stinging bite. I use my saliva to dissolve my food so I can suck it through my tube shaped mouth parts.

WHAT I LOOK LIKE: My body is dark, and less than ½ an inch. My back is oval shaped much like a boat hull, which enables me to swim on my back. I have 6 legs; 2 short front legs and my back legs are long. I carry my air supply with me as a small bubble in my shell. I have wings and fly at night because I am attracted to artificial light.

HOW I AM BORN: I go through three stages of development: egg, nymph and adult. My egg is usually attached to underwater plants. I hatch into a nymph and will molt to reach my adult form, receiving my wings in the last molt. It takes me around 6 weeks to go from egg to adult. I can live up to a year, even under ice as long as there is food and air bubbles.

FUN FACTS: Male backswimmers make a sound under water, much like a cricket, to attract female backswimmers. There are about 400 species of water backswimmers in the world.

Water Boatman (True Bug)

My Home: I am found in freshwater ponds, streams and lakes that have aquatic plants. I can fly out of the water.

What I Eat: I am primarily an herbivore. I have a soft tube shaped mouth part that I use to suck in nourishment from aquatic plants and algae. I use my saliva (spit on the food) to dissolve it so I can suck the juices back in with my soft tube mouth part. I am not able to bite.

What I Look Like: My body is dark brown or black, about ½ an inch long, an elongated shape, with short front legs that have a scoop on the end that I use to gather food. I use my long oar shaped hind legs to swim. I carry my air supply with me, under my shell. I have wings and sometimes fly at night because I am attracted to artificial lights.

How I Am Born: I go through three stages of development or incomplete metamorphosis: egg, nymph and adult. My egg is attached to underwater plants and rocks. I hatch into a nymph and will molt to reach my adult form. I receive my wings in my last molt. It takes me around 6 weeks to go from egg to adult. I can live about a year and even under ice as long as there are air bubbles.

Fun Facts: I use the air bubble I keep under my shell to breathe underwater just like a scuba diver. To keep from floating back to the surface, I have to hook my legs on a plant or rock. There are over 500 species of water boatmen in the world.

Water Strider (True Bug)

My home: I am primarily found on freshwater ponds, streams and lakes. I am able to slide along the surface of the water by distributing my weight evenly on my long legs.

What I eat: As a nymph or adult water strider, I am carnivorous and use my piercing mouth parts to suck the juices primarily from other insects or spiders, alive or dead. I find food by using my front legs to detect movement or ripple in the water and I also use my front legs to grab prey. I am considered a beneficial insect because I eat other insects including mosquito larvae.

What I look like: My body is thin, elongated, dark brown in color and about ¾ of an inch long. I have two antenna and six long thin legs. My front legs are shorter than my back legs. Some water strider species have wings.

How I am born: I go through three stages of development or incomplete metamorphosis: egg, nymph and adult. My egg is laid on aquatic plants or rocks. I hatch into a nymph and will molt many times to reach my adult form. It takes me around 8 weeks to go from egg to adult. As an adult, I usually live until a freeze, but in warmer areas I can overwinter and live up to a year.

Fun Facts: There is a water strider species that lives its entire life on the ocean. There are over 1,680 species of water striders in the world.

Yellow Jacket Wasp

MY HOME: I am aggressive and build paper nests in logs, on the sides of buildings or in trees. I am a social insect and live in colonies. Sometimes the nest populations can number in the thousands.

WHAT I EAT: I will eat other insects, but also am attracted to sweet smells as in garbage cans or will hover over your picnic table during the summer.

WHAT I LOOK LIKE: My body is yellow and black striped and I have two transparent wings. My stinger is located at the end of my abdomen.

HOW I AM BORN: I go through four stages of development: egg, larva, pupa and adult. The queen yellow jacket wasp can lay thousands of eggs. My egg is laid in an individual cell within the paper type nest. The workers in the colony take care of my egg until I hatch. The new queens hibernate over the winter and each spring builds a new colony. My average life span from egg to adult is one season.

FUN FACTS: I have a built in alarm and if attacked or killed will release a smell that alerts other wasps that come to help. Yellow jackets can sting repeatedly and are aggressive!

What Insect appears to walk on water?

Non-Insects

What looks like an insect, is not an insect and uses gills to breathe?

CENTIPEDE

MY HOME: I prefer dark, damp environments and you will find me under leaves, bark, and logs or in your basement. I am most active at night unless I am disturbed in my hiding places.

WHAT I EAT: I use my venomous jaws to catch and eat other insects, stunning or killing my prey with the poison.

WHAT I LOOK LIKE: I am flat, reddish brown in color and usually around 1 inch in length. My first pair of legs is modified venomous jaws that I use to catch other insects. If you pick me up, I may bite. I have a single pair of legs on every segment of my body.

HOW I AM BORN: I go through 2 stages of development: egg and small adult. My egg is laid in the soil during the warm summer months and the females care for my egg until I hatch. Adult centipedes will protect my egg nests. When I hatch I look just like a small adult. To grow I shed my skin which is called molting, adding a pair of legs each time I molt. I can live up to five years.

FUN FACTS: The name centipede means 'hundred legs'. In the tropical regions, some centipedes can get up to a foot long. A centipede is not an insect, it is a Chilopoda.

Millipede

MY HOME: I am found through North America and in other parts of the world that have moist environments. I live outdoors in moist, dark, protected areas like under bark, logs, leaves or rocks. I am most active at night.

WHAT I EAT: I lack the venomous front jaws of centipedes and primarily eat decaying plants.

WHAT I LOOK LIKE: I am long, slow moving, and resemble a worm. I have two pairs of legs on each body segment. A centipede has only one pair of legs on each segment. My length can be from 1 to 12 inches.

HOW I AM BORN: I go through two stages of development: egg and adult. My egg is laid in the ground during the springtime. After I hatch, I resemble a small adult. To grow, I molt and shed my skin, adding a segment and a set of legs each time my skin is shed.

FUN FACTS: They are often called 'thousand leggers', but they actually only have from 40 to 200 pair of legs. They can coil in a ball for protection and some produce a poisonous gas. There are around 10,000 species of Millipedes worldwide.

Pill Bug (Rolie Polie)

My Home: I am found in most regions of the world. I live in moist dark areas, under rocks, bark, leaves and logs.

What I Eat: I eat decaying plants or other vegetation.

What I Look Like: I have three body parts, seven pairs of legs, two antennae and two eyes. I am ¼ to ½ of an inch in length and vary in color from dark gray to white. I can roll myself into a ball when frightened and am commonly called 'Rolie Polie.'

How I Am Born: I go through two stages of development: egg and adult. The female can lay up to 100 eggs, which are held in a pouch (like a kangaroo). After about two months as an egg, I hatch and emerge as a tiny adult. I grow by molting (shedding my skin). As an adult, I can live up to three years.

Fun Facts: Pill bugs are not insects, they are crustaceans. They are related to shrimp and crayfish, breathe with gills, and need humidity or moisture to survive.

[What insect does not have a mouth?]

Checklist: What I have seen

√	Date	Name	Picture
		Ant: Common Black	
		Ant: Southern Red Fire	
		Bee: Bumble	
		Bee: Honey	
		Beetle: Click	
		Beetle: Firefly	
		Beetle: Harlequin	
		Beetle: Japanese	
		Beetle: June Bug	
		Beetle: Lady Bug	

√	Date	Name	Picture
		Boxelder (True Bug)	
		Butterfly: Cabbage	
		Butterfly: Monarch	
		Butterfly: Tiger Swallow Tail	
		Butterfly: Giant Swallowtail	
		Cicada	
		Centipede	
		Cricket	
		Dragonfly	
		Earwig: Pincher Bug	

√	Date	Name	Picture
		Fly: Crane	
		Fly: Flower	
		Fly: Horse	
		Fly: House	
		Grasshopper	
		Katydid	
		Mayfly	
		Millipede	
		Moth: Luna	
		Moth: Sphinx	

√	Date	Name	Picture
		Mosquito	
		Pill Bug (Rolie Polie)	
		Praying Mantis	
		Stink Bug: Harlequin (True Bug)	
		Walking Stick	
		Wasp: Mud Dauber	
		Wasp: Yellow Jacket	
		Water Backswimmer (True Bug)	
		Water Boatman (True Bug)	
		Water Strider (True Bug)	

GLOSSARY (1)

Ametaboly — An insect that upon hatching has almost no change (metamorphosis) in appearance, except in size, to reach their adult form. They hatch as a smaller version of their adult form.

Antennae — One of a pair of slender movable segmented sensory organs on the head of insects.

Anterior — Situated before or at the front of.

Aphid — A small sap-sucking insect (and a favorite food of ladybugs).

Arthropod — Any of a phylum (Arthropoda) of invertebrate animals (as insects, arachnids, and crustaceans) that have a segmented body and jointed appendages, a usually chitinous exoskeleton molted at intervals, and a dorsal anterior brain connected to a ventral chain of ganglia.

Brood — The young (as of a bird or insect) hatched or cared for all at one time.

Camouflage — Concealment by means of disguise.

Carnivore — Any of an order of typically flesh-eating animals, insects, or plants.

Caterpillar — The worm-like larva of a butterfly or moth.

Colony — Distinguishable localized population within a species. (Ex: colony of ants)

Chrysalis — A protecting covering: a sheltered state or stage of being or growth.

Crustacean — A group of arthropods that includes crabs, lobsters, and shrimp (and one non-insect in Bug Facts A Young Explorer's Guide).

Dorsal — Pertaining to the upper side (of insects), and the back side (of animals that walk upright).

Drones — The male of a bee (as the honeybee) that has no sting and gathers no honey. One that lives on the labors of others.

Entomologist — A zoologist that specializes in the study of insects.

Exoskeleton — An external skeleton that supports and protects an animal's/insect's body.

Ganglia — Masses of nerve cell bodies.

Gill — An organ (as of a fish) for obtaining oxygen from water.

Herbivore	A plant-eating animal, insect or organism.
Invertebrate	An animal that has no backbone.
Larva	The immature, wingless and often wormlike feeding form that hatches from the egg of many insects, alters chiefly in size while passing through several molts, and is finally transformed into a pupa or chrysalis from which the adult emerges.
Larvae	Plural. More than one larva.
Larval	The stage of a larva.
Metamorphosis	A complete change in appearance.
Molt	To shed skin.
Nectar	A sweet liquid that is secreted by a plant and is the chief raw material of honey.
Nectarivore	An animal that feeds on nectar from flowering plants.
Nymph	Any of various immature insects.
Pupa	An intermediate stage of an insect (as a bee, moth, or beetle) that occurs between the larva and adult, is usually enclosed in a cocoon or protective covering, and undergoes internal changes by which larval structures are replaced into those of the adult.
Pupal	The stage of a pupa.
Pupate	The act of transformation from pupa to adult.
Swarm	A large number of insects massed together and usually in motion.
True Bug	The Hemiptera orders of insects (around 67,000 different species) are often called True Bugs. Members of this order are distinguished from all other insects by having forewings made up of both membrane and hard portions and a proboscis (long sucking mouth tube) that is usually specialized to suck the juices from various parts of plants, although some species are predatory and are adapted to suck blood.

(1) Most sources of definition are from the Merriam - Webster Dictionary, 2012. Some modifications may have occurred for relevance to the publication material.

Reference

Division of Insects, Field Museum of Natural History, Chicago, Illinois

Clemson University, South Carolina – Entomology Extension Service Department

Florida State University, Florida – Entomology Extension Office

Iowa State University, Iowa – Entomology Extension Office

Kentucky State University, Kentucky – Entomology Extension Office

Ohio State University, Ohio – Entomology Extension Office

Royal Alberta Museum, Canada – Entomology Department

Texas A&M University, Texas – Entomology Extension Office

Virginia Polytechnic Institute and University – Cooperative Extension: Entomology

www.ingramcontent.com/pod-product-compliance
Lightning Source LLC
Chambersburg PA
CBHW061358090426
42743CB00002B/57